FAIRY TALE JOKES

Distributed to Schools and Libraries
in the United States by
ENCYCLOPAEDIA BRITANNICA EDUCATIONAL CORP.
310 S. Michigan Avenue
Chicago, Illinois 60604

Library of Congress Cataloging-in-Publication Data
Woodworth, Viki.
Fairy tale jokes / Viki Woodworth.
p. cm.
Summary: A collection of jokes and riddles
featuring such fairy tale characters as
Little Red Riding Hood, Snow White, King Arthur, and Pinocchio.
ISBN 0-89565-862-3
1. Wit and humor, Juvenile. 2. Fairy tales – Juvenile humor.
[1. Fairy tales – Wit and humor. 2. Jokes. 3. Riddles.] I. Title.
PN6163.W67 1993   91-46503
818'.5402–dc20   CIP / AC

FAIRY TALE JOKES

Compiled and Illustrated by
Viki Woodworth

THE CHILD'S WORLD

What disease did the Big Bad Wolf wish to have?

Hood-in-mouth disease.

What musician do the Big Bad Wolf and his friends love?

Wolf-gang Mozart.

Why did Little Red Riding Hood believe the Wolf's disguise?

She was hoodwinked.

What does the Big Bad Wolf eat in a restaurant?

The waiter.

What does Little Red Riding Hood become when her cape disintegrates?

Little Red Rotten Hood.

What does Little Red Riding Hood become when she leads a life of crime?
Little Red Robbing Hood.

What do you call a blonde girl with three boring men?
Goldilocks and the Three Bores.

Goldilocks: How did you dress for the party?
Little Bear: I just went bear.

How did the bear lock the little girl in the house?
With a goldi-lock.

Goldilocks: What do you need to live on?
Little Bear: Just the bear essentials.

Goldilocks: What story should I tell these lambs?
Little Bear: Goldiflocks and the Three Baas.

Why did Goldilocks feel so good?
She was feeling her oats.

What fairy tale is about pigs eating dried fruit?
The Three Little Pigs Eat Figs.

What fairy tale is about pigs eating dried fruit with a scientist?
The Three Little Pigs Eat Figs with Newton.

What fairy tale is about a rodent and a little girl who eat a lot of sugar?
Hamster and Gretel.

What fairy tale is about a rodent who loves to cook?
Hamster and Kettle.

What fairy tale is about an attractive boy and an interfering girl who eat a lot of sugar?
Handsome and Meddle.

What fairy tale is about a wolf who can't decide how to wear his hair?
The Three Little Wigs.

Arthur: What should I say to this two-headed dragon?
Merlin: Bye-bye.

Arthur: Why does that dragon have banana skins on its feet?
Merlin: They make good slippers.

What looks just like half a dragon?
The other half.

What do dragons have that nothing else has?
Baby dragons.

Why do dragons giggle whenever they walk through woods?
The trees tickle their bellies.

Merlin: Where will this dragon sleep?
Arthur: Anywhere it wants.

Why is it so hard to talk to a dragon?
The conversations just drag-on and on.

Arthur: What side of that dragon has the most scales?
Merlin: The outside.

Arthur: Why do dragons sleep in the daytime?
Merlin: Because they fight knights.

Arthur: Who is safe with this man-eating dragon around?
Merlin: The women and children!

Arthur: What is ten feet long, purple, and has two tongues?
Merlin: Gosh, I don't know, what is?
Arthur: A dragon's sneakers.

What is large, green, breathes fire and hums?

An electric dragon.

What does a bored giant say?
Fee-fie-ho-hum.

Mother: Jack, why are you going out to your garden?
Jack: To listen to my beanstalk.

Mother: How can I make a giant stew?
Jack: Keep him waiting a *very* long iime.

What two things can't a giant eat for dinner?
Breakfast and lunch.

What do you get when a giant sneezes?
Out of the way.

What does a giant say at Christmas?
Fee-fie-ho-ho-ho.

What kind of coins do foxes use?
Henny Pennies.

What did the fox think of Henny Penny?
He thought she was a little tough.

What fairy tale is about a miserly chicken who thinks the sky is falling?
Henny Penny-pincher.

What fairy tale is about a poor chicken who thinks the sky is falling?
Henny-haven't-any-Penny.

What fairy tale is about an athletic chicken who thinks the sky is falling?
Henny Tenny.

Why did the fox need an operation?
He had a henny-pendicitis attack.

What fairy tale is about a beautiful traveling whale?
Snow Whale and the Seven Wharfs.

What fairy tale is about a miserly princess who liked to eat a lot?
Snow Tight and the Seven Forks.

Wicked Queen: What kind of tea should I drink?
Snow White: Royalty.

Wicked Queen: Do you think my teeth are as sparkly as stars?
Mirror on the Wall: Yes, and they come out at night.

Wicked Queen: What should I wear in this horrible weather?
Snow White: Your reign-coat, of course.

What kind of laundry detergent did the Seven Dwarfs use?
Snow whitening and brightening.

Why did the Three Little Pigs pay the Big Bad Wolf?
For sweeping their chimney.

Can the Three Little Pigs keep a secret?
No, they squeal.

What did the Three Little Pigs have for dessert?
Pie à la mud.

What organization did the Littlest Pig join?
The Boy Snouts.

What did the Little Pig take to the laundry?
Hogwash.

What kind of wax do the Three Little Pigs use on their floors?
Boar wax.

Merlin: Let's go climb the dragon.
Arthur: Why?
Merlin: To practice our scaling.

Merlin: Let's bring the dragon on the campout.
Arthur: Why?
Merlin: So we can roast marshmallow.

Arthur: What's a dragon's favorite game?
Merlin: Don't know.
Arthur: Fireball.

How can you tell when there's a dragon in your bed?
By the "D" on his pajamas.

Why don't you see dragons in zoos?
They hide behind the garbage cans.

What kind of music does a dragon play?
Scales.

How did King Arthur see at night?
With a knight light.

Merlin: Why did you wake up?
Arthur: I had a knightmare.

What did King Arthur's hangman read?
A noosepaper.

Arthur: Did you make that rabbit disappear?
Merlin: Yes. Hare today, gone tomorrow.

What did Merlin do when young Arthur brought a dragon home to live with them?
He raised the roof.

Arthur: Why won't you jump in the water?
Merlin: I don't want to make waves.

Gepetto: What happened when you got cut?
Pinocchio: I lost a pint of sawdust.

Pinocchio: Doctor, what's the problem?
Doctor: I'm sorry to tell you this, but you have a termite-al disease.

Pinocchio: What keeps my toes attached to my feet?
Gepetto: Toe nails.

Gepetto: Why don't people like Pinocchio?
Jiminy Cricket: Well, he's a little stiff at a party and has a wooden smile.

Why won't Pinocchio go to sleep?
He's afraid of sawing logs.

What do Pinocchio and George Washington have in common?
Wooden teeth.

Cinderella: I slept in salad oil last night.
Prince Charming: Why?
Cinderella: I wanted to get up oily.

What do you get when you cross Prince Charming with a monster?
Prince Alarming.

Why did Cinderella fall down?
Because the glass slipped-her.

Coach: You're off the team!
Cinderella: But why?
Coach: You ran away from the ball.

Cinderella: How do you talk to fish?
Prince Charming: I drop them a line.

What fairy tale is about a beautiful girl who bakes bread?
Beauty and the Yeast.

What fairy tale is about a beautiful girl who goes into real estate?
Beauty and the Lease.

What fairy tale is about a beautiful girl who likes sausages?
Beauty and the Bockwurst.

What fairy tale is about a beautiful princess who spied on her friends?
Peeping Beauty.

What fairy tale is about a princess who cries a lot?
Weeping Beauty.

What fairy tale is about a conceited princess who cries a lot?
Weeping Snooty.

DATE			